grand master ● little master
series

love has many faces

Written by Patricia Merker

Illustrated by Lauren Wilhelm

Foreword

I am pleased to support and boost into form the marvelous content in this Grand Master/Little Master interactive book series.

I commend talented author Patricia Merker and the sensitive Pick-a-WooWoo publishing team for your combined commitment to bring what I consider universal, peace-making principles into the laps of children and families. This inspired book series combines soul-honoring, character-building, personal-empowerment techniques with balanced mind/body/spirit activities. The GM/LM series guides children and their families with skillful, playful fun into seeing God as our partner in life. Patricia masterfully brings story into easy living action that articulates in simple and easy-to-live ways how to create a deeply self-inspired AND Divine-inspired lifestyle.

This kind of out-of-the-box educational approach is fundamental to the internationally acclaimed NY Times best selling ***Conversations with God (CWG)*** series of books and is a mission of the School of the New Spirituality, Inc., the education non-profit founded by author and spiritual leader Neale Donald Walsch.

I'd like to highlight in a concise summary, key principles that the Grand Master/Little Master books bring to life. These foundational beliefs hold inherent power which any parent, grandparent, teacher and all youth professionals may utilize in their work and play with young people to nurture and foster healthy, joyful, loving, honored-for-who-they-are souls:

- God is the All, not any one thing outside of us
- The Divine communicates with us and inside us all the time
- Look for the spark of Source/God, or goodness, in every living being.
- Love is all there is; look inside and see.
- True Love is unconditional, that is it remains without conditions.
- What you CAUSE in the world comes back to you, CAUSE something wonderful today
- Every minute has choice in it. Choose the best for the good of you and for the good of all.
- There is no right or wrong, life is – and we live, learn to love through it all
- Raising children with the belief that they are perfect, magnificent souls on earth will change the world – one healthy child at a time.

As a decade-long co-leader of the School of the New Spirituality, Inc, I professionally endorse Patricia's books. Thank you, Patricia and Pick-a-WooWoo, for this important educational series and contribution to our world.

Linda Lee Ratto EdM, Former Director, Global Education; School of the New Spirituality, Founded by Neale Donald Walsch.

A note from the Author

The Grand Master/Little Master series of books teach, even very young children, about their source of power within. Your child will delight as they follow the journey of the "chosen" little masters in each story. There is no shortage of smiles, admiration and compassion that will warm their hearts and inspire them to re-read these stories over and over.

If however, you choose to take these magical stories to the next level, so begins an interactive adventure in which your child becomes the main character. Minimal parental participation and weekly lessons from Grand Master allow children to address their *own* childhood fears, concerns and self esteem issues.

Universal Laws are presented in ways that give children an opportunity to *experience* their magic rather than to simply read about it. To access the interactive unit of this series which includes how to get started, a synopsis of the lesson associated with each story, a note to the parents, and the weekly lessons from Grand Master to your child, please visit http://www.pickawoowoo.com/childrens-spiritual-books/grand-master-little-master-series/

Enjoy the journey!

Patricia Merker

Patricia can be contacted through her website
http://www.thegrandmasterlittlemasterseries.com/

Jordan tossed and turned in his bed. He knew it was way past his bedtime, but how could he be expected to sleep? Tomorrow was the first day of school and so many things were running wild in his brain!

He had a brand new yellow backpack with cool designs on it. Dad took him shopping and let him pick it out all by himself. He had some pretty terrific pencils in neon colors, three folders that already had his name on them, two notebooks, crayons, glue stick and best of all, a fluorescent yellow box with his favorite cartoon characters all over it to hold his school supplies. Could it get any better than this?

His big sister, Haley, told him that first grade was harder than Kindergarten. He didn't care. He loved to learn. Jordan knew that he was pretty smart for his age. His mom always told people that when he was just 1 ½ years old he would pick up plastic alphabet letters and in his tiny voice would say, "etter b", and then drop them into a bucket. He could even count to almost 1000, with only just a little bit of help.

Learning was fun. Sometimes it seemed that he just couldn't get enough. And the computer, well, that was his favorite.

He yawned and decided that if he didn't go to sleep soon, he might as well get dressed and go have breakfast!

There was so much noise and confusion in the classroom when he arrived at school! His belly felt all nervous and jittery. The kids were happily buzzing around and saying hello to each other after a long summer. Almost everyone from Kindergarten was in his class again this year. There were only a few kids that he didn't recognize.

He took a seat next to Keaton and they talked about what their new teacher might look like. Would she be pretty? Would she smell nice like Miss Robinson, their Kindergarten teacher last year? Would she have a pretty smile? Keaton was Jordan's very best friend. It seemed like they had always known each other.

Jordan had always been the teacher's pet. He knew he wasn't supposed to say it out loud because some of the other children might think he was bragging. Or, maybe they would feel sad because they wished they could be special to the teacher like he was. He felt bad for the other kids but he felt lucky for himself. After all, teachers seemed to like the kids who knew the answers and Jordan certainly knew the answers.

Last year, Miss Robinson let Jordan help her clean the blackboard anytime that he wanted. She couldn't always pick on him to help pass out birthday cupcakes, but she did it a lot. More than the other kids, Jordan thought. He enjoyed talking with her about things and she always seemed so interested in him.

Jordan knew that not just anyone could be a teacher. You had to be special.

When I grow up, Jordan thought, I'll be a teacher and make someone feel special.

An elderly woman walked into the room and put some things on the desk. Jordan knew that she could not be his teacher because she didn't look friendly. Maybe she was a cafeteria lady. Yes, that must be it! She was way too grumpy looking to be a teacher. And she wasn't smiling. She was also way too old to be a teacher, Jordan was sure of it. And if he had to guess, he thought she might not smell as good as Miss Robinson. However, she certainly looked like she was preparing to stay . . .

The woman stood in the front of the room and said in a scratchy voice, "Good morning class, welcome to first grade." She didn't smile.

"Everyone please be quiet and find a seat", she continued. "My name is Mrs. Conner and we will begin roll call in just a moment, when everyone gets quiet."

Jordan thought he might throw up. Seriously throw up.

He stared in disbelief, waiting for her to say, "Just kidding, I'm really the cafeteria lady!" He was certain it was all just a big mistake.

"Please don't make me write your name on a list of children who misbehave on the first day of school!" Mrs. Conner said, raising her voice in a cackling sort of way. And she stood in the front of the room, her arms folded across her chest, waiting for the children to obey. She didn't smile.

The kids got very quiet. It was as if every one of them knew, in an instant, that Kindergarten was over.

She began roll call. "Here", called Susanna. "Here" said Trevor. "Here" yelled Claire. "Here" whispered a very sad Jordan, wishing he wasn't.

If she would just smile, maybe she would be prettier. She might even smell nicer. Yes, he was sure of it. If she would just smile . . .

But she didn't. Four miserable months went by and she didn't smile. Not a real smile anyway. Sometimes the edges of her mouth turned up a little as though she wanted us to *think* that she was smiling, but she wasn't.

It was pretty obvious to Jordan that Mrs. Conner didn't like children. He suspected that she particularly didn't like him, but he didn't know why.

"Hey Jordan", yelled Keaton from across the playground one afternoon at recess. "I figured out why Mrs. Conner doesn't smile. She doesn't have any teeth!" They both giggled. At least he had Keaton. He was feeling pretty empty these days but at least he still had his best friend.

But Jordan really missed sitting next to Keaton. In nursery school, where they met, their teacher let them sit next to each other. Miss Robinson put them together too because she knew they were best friends. Mrs. Conner thought that the two of them together were troublemakers and they needed to be separated. But they weren't troublemakers. They hated to get in trouble.

Jordan was sad and he knew that Mrs. Conner had no interest whatsoever in how he felt about his best friend.

One day Bobby, the class bully, kept smacking Jordan with a rubber band from behind him in the seat. Jordan let out a loud "ouch!" when the rubber band stung him on his back. Mrs. Conner walked over, grabbed Jordan's wrist and sternly said, "Young man, it is very difficult to teach when thoughtless children make noise and clammer around. I want you to be quiet or next time it's to the principal's office!"

"But Mrs. Conner, I didn't . . ."

"QUIET! She shouted, and walked away. The class stared at him. Jordan choked back a sob. No one had ever been so mean to him. No one had ever disliked him so much. What's wrong with me? Jordan wondered.

That afternoon, he got off the bus and just like every other day he walked up the driveway to his house. As always, his mom was standing there to greet him. She could tell something was terribly wrong. She got down on her knees and opened her arms up wide. Jordan walked in the door, dropped his books and papers on the floor, and ran into his mom's open arms. He cried like he had never cried before. It was as if he had been holding this sob since the first day of school.

"I hate her, mom! She's the meanest person in the whole world and she hates kids, especially me!" Jordan cried, tears soaking his shirt and drenching his mom's heart.

"Please don't make me go back to school."

Jordan rolled over in his bed and stretched. It was Saturday and there was no school. No Mrs. Conner; no one to make him feel bad. Today he could pretend that everything was okay.

His mom and dad promised that they would talk to the principal but Jordan said it would only make things worse. She would still be mean to him in other ways. It was best if they didn't.

Feeling very resigned, he put his pillow over his head. Something was under there; what was it? A paper; a letter, to him! He pulled it out and began to read.

Dear Little Master,

It is time that we met, you and I. Your sister has learned to look in her heart when she begins to feel separate from me. You must now learn that too. Soon it will be the job of you and your sister to spread the word to every child. I live in them all. They are all Little Masters. But for now we must work on an important lesson. There is something that you must know:

I am but a breath away and I am the voice of your soul. Never look to others to see how you feel about yourself, Little Master. Look into your heart, and you will know the Truth. Your heart never lies. You are Love, Perfection, and pure Joy. Do not listen to anyone that says you are not.

When an adult is mean to a child, it is not because there is something wrong with the child! You see, when a person cannot see beauty, joy and perfection in another person, it is because they do not see beauty, joy and perfection in themselves. It is very difficult to love another when you cannot love yourself. When one cannot laugh, it is because they are sad inside.

I live in the soul of every living being. See if you can find a way, Little Master, to find that spark of me in your teacher. I promise you, I am there. This might take patience and hard work, but you are a Little Master in training. Patience and hard work is good.

If you find a glint of a smile in your teacher, you have found me. Do something nice or make her feel special. Try to find a way for her to love herself, even if it is for just a moment. You cannot change her life. Only she can do that. But you, Little Master, can let her see herself through your eyes.

Love is all there is Little Master. Sometimes it does not look like love, but it is. I am love; I am you; I am the world and I live inside the soul of every living being. See if you can find me in everyone and everything! Do not ever forget that I am always with you, *even when you think that I am not.*

I love you.

Grand Master

Jordan had heard Haley talk about Grand Master but he thought she was crazy! Is Grand Master real? Jordan thought. Does Grand Master live inside me too?

Jordan wasn't sure about any of that right now but he did know one thing for sure. He felt good inside. Better than he had felt in a long time and he didn't care if Grand Master was real or not. He had known all along that he was okay. At least, in his heart he knew. He was determined to see if he could make Mrs. Conner smile; a real smile. Not the kind of pretend smiles she did everyday that weren't real. But an honest to goodness genuine smile!

It wasn't an easy job, being a Little Master. It meant seeing things differently than almost everyone else! Jordan shared his secret with Keaton, but only because they had been best friends for so long. Anyone else would think he was crazy. Jordan suspected that Keaton thought he was crazy too, but was too nice to say so.

They thought about drawing a picture to give to Mrs. Conner. They tried to write a song for her but that was way too hard, and besides, it sounded so funny that they couldn't stop laughing! Maybe if they bought her some perfume? Nah, that's no good. What would make her love herself? And then they had a brainstorm. Valentines Day was about to arrive. Valentines Day is love! They knew exactly what they would do.

The day before their Valentines party, on the playground, Jordan and Keaton gave every child a red, construction paper, homemade heart. Each child had to write one thing that made Mrs. Conner special to them. This was not an easy task and it took at least half of recess to accomplish this! There were a few kids, of course, who would not participate. Jordan wasn't sure he blamed them. All of the little hearts went inside a decorated box and were ready for delivery at the party tomorrow.

When the party officially began the next day, Jordan walked up to Mrs. Conner's desk. She was grading papers and didn't seem to want to be bothered.

"Mrs. Conner?" Jordan said softly.

"What do you want Jordan?" she said without looking up.

"The class has something special for you. We don't know for sure if you'll like it, or if you'll want to keep it, cause we know you think we misbehave too much. We hope you like it anyway."

"The class made something for *me*?" she asked disbelievingly.

Mrs. Conner looked up from her papers and into Jordan's eyes. He thought he saw a softness that wasn't there before.

"Is this a good time to give it to you?" Jordan asked.

"Yes, I believe it is. I'd like that very much," replied Mrs. Conner.

"Okay, I'll be right back!" Jordan said enthusiastically. And with that, he ran to the back of the room to retrieve the pink box.

A hush came over the children. Everyone was anxious to see if Mrs. Conner would like her gift. Jordan thought that Mrs. Conner looked prettier already. For the first time ever, he thought, she looked like a nice lady. It was as though no one had done anything special for her, at least not in a long, long time.

He sat the box in front of her. All the children ran up and circled her desk. Very carefully, she took off the lid and peered into the box full of red hearts. A smile crept across her face; *a real smile!* "There it is!" Jordan thought. He was filled with a warm, wonderful feeling, as though everything was right in the world, and he had somehow played a part in it.

"Read the hearts, Mrs. Conner! Read the hearts!" shouted the class.

Mrs. Conner picked up the hearts, one by one, and read them out loud:

I love you becaus you let us do sum of our homworc in class and I have moor time to play at home.
Frum, Jimmy

I love you because you dress pretty.
Love, Sara

I love you because you are good at teaching math. Its my favrit subject!
From Tommy

Mrs. Conner continued to read all the valentines, one by one, until she read them all. She looked up, tears welling in her eyes, and in a voice that almost no one could hear, said "Thank you. This is the nicest thing anyone has ever done for me. I'll always remember this."

"I couldn't fit what I wanted to say on one of those little red hearts," Jordan said to Mrs. Conner, "so, I wrote mine on a piece of paper. It's not as pretty as the others though."

"I'll bet its wonderful Jordan, can I see it?"

"Sure" he replied.

Mrs. Conner unfolded the paper that Jordan handed to her. It had smudges and eraser marks all over it. It had two red crayon colored hearts drawn and colored in. It read:

Dear Mrs. Conner,

I know its not too easy being a teacher to all us little kids. Sometimes we don't listen and we're very noisy and messy. But I know that God only picks special people to be teachers. So if you get sad sometimes and think that we're not learning anything that you teach us, you are wrong. You are helping us grow into adults and we learn from you about what's important. You have taught me to look into someone's insides to see what is special about them. I think that sometimes things happen to us when we start to get big and sometimes it makes us sad and we stay that way for a long time. When you get real sad, remember that God gave you to us and you are special. HAPPY VALENTINES DAY,

Love, Jordan

P.S. My mom helped me spell this but all the words are mine.

Mrs. Conner could barely choke out the last word. She reached out and put her arms around Jordan.

"If anything that I have done has helped you to be the special, loving little boy that you are, then indeed I am blessed" she said, "and do you know something special?" she asked, "I learned a great deal from *you* today. I think God picked you to be *my* teacher. I guess we're both pretty lucky!"

"Yeah, I guess we are" replied Jordan, and he felt happy.

Jordan awoke the next morning and he felt wonderful. He knew that he had found the spark in Mrs. Conner that Grand Master had referred to. And he was responsible in some way. He had made a difference in someone else's life. What a powerful thing to feel! Imagine, she called him a teacher! It was probably one of the nicest feelings he had ever had.

Once again, under his pillow there was a piece of paper. He had a very good idea who it was from. The letter read:

Dear Little Master,

Congratulations, you have learned your lesson well. I am very proud of all your hard work. You are going to be a very wise Little Master, indeed!

Never forget this lesson. It is an important one. When someone does not behave in a way that is kind, joyful or loving, it is only because they do not know how. It has nothing to do with you, Little Master, even though it might look and feel like it. Maybe they have a broken heart, maybe they are angry or maybe they have no one to love. What you see is the best kind of love that they are able to show. I know it's hard to believe, but Love is all there is! It simply shows up in different forms. But this is something that a Little Master has to look for and sometimes it's not easy. It is also important to understand that you can't help everyone. If you feel that someone is dangerous, stay away or ask for help. Their behavior has <u>nothing</u> to do with you, no matter what it looks like.

But for most, if you can look for the good and let them see themselves through your eyes, you are a teacher in its highest form. Trust that the Universe sent them to you for a purpose. You, my Little Master, did that yesterday.

Do not forget that when you need me, I am only a breath away. Stop, close your eyes and feel the warmth of me in your heart. That is where I live. I am part of you and you are part of me. We cannot be separated. I am always with you, even when you think I am not.

I love you, Grand Master

Jordan folded Grand Masters letter and put it close to his heart so he could be closer than close to this wonderful new discovery; this Grand Master that lived in his heart and soul, that was part of him.

Has he always been inside of me, and I just didn't know? Jordan wondered. But almost before he could finish his thought, the answer was there, this time with no letter.

"I have always been a part of you, Little Master. I have always been just a breath away."

Jordan smiled at the thought and rolled over wondering what his next lesson would be.

© Copyright 2011

The right of Patricia Merker to be identified as the Author and Lauren Wilhelm to be identified as the Artist of the work has been asserted by them in accordance with the Copyright, Designs and Patents Act 1988. All rights reserved. No part of this book may be used or reproduced, stored in a retrieval system, or transmitted in any form, or by any means electronic, mechanical, recording, photocopying, or in any manner whatsoever without permission in writing from the publisher, except for book reviews.

National Library of Australia Cataloguing-in-Publication entry
Author –Merker, Patricia,
Title: Love has many faces / by Patricia Merker; Illustrated by Lauren Wilhelm
Edition: 1st ed.
ISBN 9781921883095 (pbk.)
Series: Merker, Patricia. Grand master, little master; bk. 3
Other Contributors: Wilhelm, Lauren
Dewey Number A8234

Publishing Details
Published in Australia - Pick-A-Woo Woo Publishers
www.pickawoowoo.com

Printed
Lightning Source (US/UK/EUR/AUS)

Channels / Distribution

United States
Ingram Book Company; Amazon.com; Baker & Taylor

Canada
Chapters Indigo; Amazon Canada

United Kingdom
Amazon.com; Bertrams; Book Depository Ltd; Gardners; Mallory International

Australia

DA Information Services; The Nile; Emporium Books Online; James Bennet (Australian Libraries)
Dennis Jones and Associates; Brumby Books and Music

Other Books in the Grand Master Little Master Series

**Book One
The Karate Tournament
Meet Grand Master
Topic: Cause and Effect**

Grand Master says:
"What you *CAUSE* in the world comes back to you
Little Master. *CAUSE* something wonderful today!"

The Karate Tournament is the first book and the foundation for all subsequent books in *The Grand Master/Little Master series*. This book is your child's introduction to Grand Master and his/her invitation to go on a life-changing adventure!

When eight-year-old Haley's mother asks her if she would like to play a game on the morning of her karate tournament, she is somewhat reluctant, given all the butterflies in her stomach! Not quite able to resist the temptation, however, she agrees. Grand Master (who makes His/Her presence known through mom in this first story) tells Haley that she has been chosen to be a Little Master-in-training and there is much to do. What follows is a heart warming story of a little girl who learns the importance and magic of Cause and Effect; what goes around, comes around. "What you put out in the world comes back, Little Master; cause love, cause kindness, cause forgiveness. Try not to cause sadness or anger. This too, must come back." This is the story of Haley, and how she turns a very scary and nervous situation into a joyous occasion by her conscious use of Law.

**Book Two
Sink or Swim
Topic: Fear**

Grand Master says:
"Everyone has fear at some time in his or her life, Little Master. The choice is whether you have IT or it has YOU.
Choose one, because it *truly* is a choice!"

Sink Or Swim is the second book in *The Grand Master/Little Master series* and addresses the topic of fear. It is highly recommended that you begin this series with *The Karate Tournament*, which is the foundation for all subsequent books in the series, and allows your child to meet Grand Master and be chosen to be a "little master-in-training". It is not necessary to follow in order after book one.

Whatever your child may be afraid of: the dark, heights, monsters in the closet, or flying, etc., they will relate to Haley's crippling fear of the water, and what it costs her to hang on to the fear. This book gives your child an opportunity to observe their fear differently. Both adults and children will find themselves asking the question "Is this fear something that I have, or does this fear have me?

www.ingramcontent.com/pod-product-compliance
Lightning Source LLC
Chambersburg PA
CBHW042250100526
44587CB00002B/86